Life Seasons

poems by

Gail Lipe

Finishing Line Press
Georgetown, Kentucky

Life Seasons

Copyright © 2025 by Gail Lipe
ISBN 979-8-88838-961-4 First Edition
All rights reserved under International and Pan-American Copyright Conventions. No part of this book may be reproduced in any manner whatsoever without written permission from the publisher, except in the case of brief quotations embodied in critical articles and reviews.

ACKNOWLEDGMENTS

Picnic in the Woods, I Swam With the Rain Today, The River of Emotion, and What are You Going to Leave This World were previously self-published in a pocket book chapbook titled *No Other Choice: Nature Calls.*

Publisher: Leah Huete de Maines
Editor: Christen Kincaid
Cover Art: Gail Lipe
Author Photo: Tracy Grochow
Cover Design: Elizabeth Maines McCleavy

Order online: www.finishinglinepress.com
also available on amazon.com

Author inquiries and mail orders:
Finishing Line Press
PO Box 1626
Georgetown, Kentucky 40324
USA

Contents

Nurture (Summer)
- Passing Thought 1
- Biography of Our Lives 2
- Architect of Our Lives 3
- A Moment Stopped 4
- Another World 6
- I Swam with the Rain Today 7
- Real Love 9
- Sleeping Child 10
- Right Where I Belong 11
- What is Happiness? 12
- My Body is Not Me 13
- Holding Pattern 14
- Disappearing Details 15

Loss (Fall)
- The Gathering 19
- Forever Changed 20
- My Aloneness 21
- Understanding 22
- Beside Her 24
- How are You Really Doing? 26
- Mortality 28
- the gift 29

Darkness (Winter)
- Tears Won't Come 33
- The River of Emotion 34
- Seed of Destruction 36
- When Will it Stop 37
- Insanity 38
- Sanity and Survival 40

Hope (Spring)
- A Place of Acceptance 43
- elders' wisdom 44

Comfortable Place of Sameness 45
Looking Forward 46
Application Makes the Difference 47
The Quiet Time Between 48
A Beautiful Day 49
Picnic in the Woods 50
My Sanctuary 51
Beauty of Perceptions 52
Home 53
What are You Going to Leave this World? 55

*Will I leave the world
a better place
because I was here?*

Nuture (Summer)

Passing Thought

A thought trickled through my brain today.
Like a shadow, it didn't stay,
and it didn't grow.
It just trickled, trickled slow.
A drop here and a drop there,
gathering they did not dare.
For a pool of thought would create
the need to contemplate.

Biography of Our Lives

Memories are God's strings
that knit us together.
You are gone.
You are with me.
The string of memories
keeps us connected.

Memories are a gift.
They have the power
to lift us up,
or tear us down.
They make us feel
and learn.

Memories have
the magic of healing.
The magic is not
always positive.
What created the memories
helped create us.

Memories can create
who we show to the world.
They can make us
guarded or vulnerable,
quiet or talkative,
quarrelsome or compassionate.

Memories are
the biography
of our lives.
They tell our story,
and remind us
how far we've come.

Architect of Our Lives

Choices.
Each day
there are choices
to be made.
Minor or major,
each choice
affects
the outcome
of a situation,
a day, or a life.

A domino effect.

We choose
how we see the world,
our priorities,
who we love,
how we love,
where we live,
where we work,
how we treat others,
how we behave.

Choice,
the architect
of our lives.
What choices
are you
making today?

A Moment Stopped

Water droplet imprints
on my glasses.
The sky swollen with
dark gray clouds.
I smile.
Inside my heart dances
as mist washes away
the drabness
and consistency
of life.

The slats sigh
resistance
as I step onto
the boardwalk.
Ripples on the lake
slap each other
as they run away
from raindrops.

Drought exposed
thick, soft muck
lines the bank.
Colorful leaves create
underwater paintings.

A mallard and his mate
swim closer
then away
then closer
looking for food,
unable to decide if
I am a threat.

A small muskrat
swims away
from the silt plume
created by the spring
rushing to feed

the bathtub lake,
a hollow fallen tree
his home.

Unexpected pleasure
amidst the busy.
Accepting the gift
I stop.

Another World

Stepping into the grove, the pine trees tower over me.
A thick bed of pine needles blanket the ground
with only a few blades of grass daring to emerge,
scattered in groups as if to say "together we are strong."
I entered a different world
through an invisible door.
The air is different here.
It is charged with an energy that nearly takes my breath away.

Sitting on the bed of needles, a tall pine at my back,
I breathe in the amazing energy.
Above is a green canopy, with splashes of blue sky peeking through.
The sun filters down, kissing the ground with dots
of brightness throughout the floor,
ever changing in the breeze.

They are here.
I can almost see the fairies dancing around the pine trees,
the bed of brown pine needles beneath their naked feet,
wings twittering on their backs
glistening in the filtered sunlight
while giggles cascade all around them.
Watching the curious dance, I can hear the flute and lyre.
The beat is broken regularly with a "tag, you're it"
or a laugh, or some juicy gossip.

This place of healing is a gift,
a gift from God to feed the soul.
As I turn to God, the fairies sit down around me.
Their energy changes from whimsical playfulness
to reverence and respect.
A soft understanding
flows through the grove.

My heart feels the energy.
My mind allows me to stop.
My soul is fed.

I Swam With the Rain Today

Perched on a stone stool
under a grass hut
near the pool
I heard the gentle rain
softly kiss the trees.
Bright yellow birds,
the size of a spring robin,
chased each other
in a pattern mimicking
a corkscrew roller coaster.

Rain drops danced
on the pool's surface
playing a symphony
with their pings,
an invitation to join them.
"Why not?
I'm going to get wet anyway."
Stripping off extra clothing
I headed toward the pool.

Laughing at me
the rain stroked my hair,
but I washed it away
as I plunged into the pool.
Soft and light, the rain
accompanied me
as I swam from one side
to the other
and back again.
By the third lap,
more raindrops
joined the dance,
falling straight down.

Rain is different here.
Clouds can dump buckets
but the drops
are still soft and light.

Standing in the middle
my chin barely under water,
eyes a few inches
above the surface,
I watched the raindrops bounce
as they hit the pool,
dancing in perfect choreography.
"Hey! Hey!"
Umbrella in hand,
two young security guards
ran toward the pool
to usher me out of the water.
"It is for your safety."

Asked if they had ever
watched rain drops dance,
they didn't understand.

Real love

I want a love that flows
like rain off a flowers gown
soaking deep into the earth
giving life to the soul
and beauty to the spirit.

I want a love that has no bounds
like the eagle soaring higher
and higher without thought of
insecurity or failure.

I want a love that is foolish and giddy
like the laughter of mischievous children
joy echoing from every sound
bringing happiness to the heart.

I want a love that returns
like metal responding to a magnet
feeling the energy invested
replying with a willingness to connect.

I want a love that has its ups and downs
like the roaring waves of the ocean
never dieing, potency increasing
the inner structure constant
as the outer parts take on the trials of daily life.

I want a love that is real.

Sleeping Child

I lay here
listening
to the steady rhythm
of your breathing
Dreams
taking you away
from me
Alone
in love

Right Where I Belong

I am a butterfly
flitting from project to project
the nectar of one not satisfying
I am a woman
alone and capable
I am blue and green,
red and purple
I am colorful
with the many facets of me
I am beautiful
in my way.

I am stalled
at a crossroad
I am chaotic
not knowing
which direction I should choose
I am afraid
to move forward
I am existing
where I am

I am craving nature
to nurture my soul
I am letting go
of old anchors
I am believing
that I am good enough

I am trusting
one step in front
of another
I am ok
with where I am
I am right
where I belong

What is Happiness?

Happiness
doesn't exist.
It's a myth created
for consumerism.

Expecting continual happiness
is unrealistic,
life challenges get in the way.

But happiness
does exist
inside us, in moments.

It cannot be
bought, or stolen,
or consumed.

Happiness
is an emotional statement
of joy, satisfaction,
contentment,
which can only come
from within.

It comes from
how we see ourselves,
and the world around us,
from being OK
with where we are,
knowing we are
right where we
belong.

My Body is not Me

You see my body.
My body is not me.

It is a borrowed vehicle,
like a rented car.
A vessel housing me,
a gift allowing me
to experience life,
along with its blessings
and its sorrows.

I am a transient guest,
the caretaker of this body.
If you look farther
I am visible.
You will see me
shining through.

Holding Pattern

I am in a holding pattern
hovering above my life,
waiting
to respect myself
   to live each day
procrastinating until
the time is right
but that time never comes
when I am old
I will travel
I will write
I will create...
But I am old now.

Disappearing Details

She walks down the street
oblivious to her surroundings.
Flower petals grab at her
from the red blanket under her feet,
unable to get her attention
from the day's missions
consuming her mind

The cascading flower buds
in the unlikely tree
have become part
of her familiar environment,
a detail disappearing
into the fabric of her life.

Not long ago,
when she was new
to this place,
she would have stopped
to admire the beauty
and complexity
of the flowers in the tree.

Where does that awe
and curiosity go
when familiarity moves in?
Why do we wait
for something to change
before we slow down
and notice the details?

Loss (Fall)

The Gathering

As dusk fell
and pink, purple and deep blue
filled the sky,
honking,
that sounded like chaos,
drew me to the gathering,
not on a hill,
but on a lake,
the water blanketed with
hundreds of geese,
excitement heard
in their conversations.
In the organized chaos
it was as if
orders were barked,
arguments started,
discussion of the
southward journey
soon to be embarked on
took place—
      Which way do we go?
      Who flies point?
A family of seven lifted
off the water headed one way,
honking their salutations.
      Safe journey.
      Avoid the hunters.
Minutes later, a family of five
flew off in another direction.
Family groups continued
to take turns flying away
until the lake was bare.
The final family reunion
of the season.

Forever Changed

Life was forever changed
        words not making sense
                justifying actions
                        disbelief
      family fractured
            trust destroyed
                    divorce
      went to trial
            found guilty
                  prison time

Life was forever changed
      I now live alone
            freedom to live
                  or hibernate
      support myself
            love my children
                  they love me
      God's taken care of me
            found blessings
                  trust in Him

Life was forever changed
      it's hard sometimes
            empty house
                  maintenance
      learning about me
            about the past
                  self grace

Life is forever changed

My Aloneness

Growing comfortable in my aloneness
no one to interrupt me
or need me
or make my choices for me

growing comfortable in my aloneness
gives me independence
gives me the ability to move on
gives me a chance to grow

too comfortable in my aloneness
no one to talk to
or help with chores
or bounce around ideas with

pulling away in my aloneness
rejecting family gatherings
and grandkid time
and group events

becoming a hermit in my aloneness
raises anxiety levels
and despair
and increases food intake

beware of being too comfortable in my aloneness
of pulling away in my aloneness
of becoming a hermit in my aloneness
of destroying contentment in my aloneness

Understanding

The scope is done.

Staring into space,
his hands reach for something
in the empty air.
"There are so many of them."
Things I cannot see.
Are angels surrounding him,
sent by the many prayers offered for his health and comfort?

He takes my hand,
fingers in one hand, wrist in the other,
drawing me nearer,
staring through me.
A penetrating, unnerving stare,
as if he sees my very soul.
Is he seeing my aura?

"Are you the one who drives the bus?" he asks.
"No."
Seconds slip by as he holds my hand, staring.
"Where are you?" I ask.
"I'm at school."
He's actually in a hospital bed after jerking awake,
arms and legs flying in the air as his whole body jumped off the bed.

Changing positions, he is moved to a chair,
hooked up to wires and tubes.
He is a fall risk.
"I guess I can take this home with me," he said
holding the heart monitor as he stands,
beepers sounding.

"Where are you going?" I ask later as the man stands.
"To take this back where I got it," he said
holding the catheter tube,
beepers again announcing his escape plan.

And so the morning went.
This fiercely independent man, now fragile,
his body more frail than he realizes,
his mind often confused.
He is not understanding the help he needs,
yet it may be us not understanding
all that he can do.

Beside Her

We sit in silence
holding hands,
one ancient,
one old.

She asks about me.
I talk about work.
"I love pickled liver."
"What made you think
of pickled liver?"
"I thought that's what you said."
I stop talking.
Linear conversation is hard.

I am old.
She is my mother,
residing between reality
and a world within her,
hearing things
that are not said,
believing things
that are not meant.

She is dying,
slowly,
struggling to breathe.
She is afraid.
Afraid of the unknown
    of the suffering to come
      of dying
        of dying alone.

"I will be ok," she says.
"Will you be ok?"
She worries about me.
"Yes."
"Are you ready?" I ask.
"Yes. Are you?"
"Yes."

Back and forth
between fear
and acceptance.
Fear ultimately wins.

We sit in silence
holding hands,
one ancient,
one old,
remembering.

How Are You Really Doing?

"How are you really doing?"
A simple question,
you would think.

How do I tell her
that a full parking lot
at the store
often scares me?

"I can do this. I can do this.
I can do this."

My mantra as I enter the store.

How do I tell her
that panic sets in
at the most inopportune times,
like when I can't find the candy canes?

"I can do this."

How do I tell her
that one minute I'm fine
and the next thing I know
I'm struggling to keep my composure?

"I can do this."

How do I tell her
that her dying was hard,
and her having COVID
and how it affected my work
was hard,
and then her getting better
and me going back to work
was hard?

"How are you really doing?"

"OK. The last month has been a struggle, but I'm OK."

Mortality

Wearing black
I sit alone
on a black chair.
A black cloud within me
strains to retain its water.
Unsuccessful, my eyes
begin to leak
        for my friend
                for his family
                       for me.
No!
I will it to stop.

Surrounded by strangers,
some I know.
I do not belong.

Stories begin
joy, laughter, sadness.
I have no stories
only respect

Mortality settles in,
I am alone.

the gift

bitter sweet
today
death, wedding
mourning, joy
acceptance, sadness

she is dieing
a few months to live
accepting the future
sad to leave
to miss the wedding,
to miss grandchild gracing
a kindergarden classroom

the wedding
is moved
seven weeks away
a regret diverted
a gift given

Darkness (Winter)

Tears Won't Come

I am lost
tears back up
behind the damn
of my resolve

Keep on keeping on
be strong
the Lord only gives
what you can handle

The ache
of uncried tears
builds pressure
challenging the damn

The damn should burst
I'm too exhausted
I want to cry
the tears won't come

The River of Emotion

Today is good
I'm good enough
      confident
      content
      competent
One day

Today is scarey
I panic
      failure
      frustration
      fear
The next day

Up and down
day by day.
Panic and calm
trade places
on a whim
without consulting me.

Emotions
I am unable
to control.
At times I basque
in their inconsistencies,
wondering
where they
come from.

I step outside
my body,
analyzing.
The river
of emotion
flows over me
as I search
for the drop
of where it began.

Sometimes
I can find it.
Only sometimes.
More often
I swim with
the river,
confused,
seeking the calm.

Seed of Destruction

I am small,
a seed of
destruction.
I cannot seem
to bloom.
My plant
becomes thorns,
my foliage
turns to razors.
I am
unpleasant
to look at,
painful
to touch.
I try to
wrap love
around others.
It cuts
and hurts,
slashing away
bits and pieces
of my soul.

When Will it Stop?

Too much
Overwhelmed
When will it stop?

I suppose
when the darkness comes
as the casket closes
and the dirt strikes
a rhythm on top
as it is buried.

That's when
the challenges end
and peace
permeates the soul.

But does it?
What work will God
give to me then?
Will it be a break
or more challenging
than on earth?

Insanity

I feel my sanity slipping away
dripping away
as the neural pathways disintegrate

disconnection
not catching things
crumbling emotionally

trapped
tired
a little girl
cowering in a corner
with an invisible blaze
surrounding me
the blaze of emotional stress

manipulated
lied to
used and abused

Fight…
Flight…
Don't let the flames devour you

it's hard
I'm tired
rest, peace,
rejuvenation, solitude
but it's so hard

the blaze closes in
closer
closer

Fight. Fight!

the flames recede a little.
I'm tired
the flames return

Fight. Fight!

again I am not consumed
but the flames are all around me
constantly
unyielding
unforgiving

I'm tired
the flames rage and crowd me
until their fingers poke
at my hair and clothing

Fight...

I'm tired
I can't
the flame devours me
leaving a disconnected,
        disoriented,
                unintelligible
                      being

Sanity and Survival

Sanity
and survival
go hand in hand,
and sanity
is a fickle thing.
When survival
crowds out
creativity,
sanity
whittles away.

Hope (Spring)

A Place of Acceptance

And we talked,
like the Saturday mornings
I used to cherish.
Quiet time,
just the two of us,
talking about anything
and everything,
healing for one or both of us.
This morning,
our conversation
brought me
to a place of acceptance.

I was trying to
hang on to people,
where we were in the past,
afraid to lose the love
and relationship.
Changes causing fear
of getting old,
of being alone.
Afraid to let go
of what was
to build something new.

elders' wisdom

naïve innocence
a rainbow world
love fixes everything
the view of young eyes

amidst the rainbows
mistakes recycle
unexpected hurts
love binds, forgives

elders' wisdom
a rainbow world
through grace
the view of older eyes

Comfortable Place of Sameness

I'm in a comfortable place of sameness,
ideas and hopes hidden,
enveloped in tomorrow.
Change creates internal chaos.

If I create a wellness vision,
put my ideas and dreams
in front of me,
can that pull them out
of the envelope of fantasy
and into reality?

Looking Forward

Lying in bed in the quiet of the night,
decompressing from the day
contemplating
I realized the present
is where I want to stay.

Reliving the past again and again
is not where I want to be.
Looking forward to the future
from this point in time
is really what suits me.

Application Makes the Difference

A thought,
an idea,
turns to intention,
to a plan,
but without
application
nothing happens.

Application
turns the thought
into reality.

The Quiet Time Between

The balcony door creaks open,
letting the cool breath of morning air
filter into the bedroom.
Silence fills the backyard
as its inhabitants wait
for the sun to rise.
It is early,
the quiet time between
the skittering and rummaging
of the night critters,
and the awakening
of the birds and squirrels.
My favorite part of the day,
where time stops,
if only for a moment,
before the rest of the world
wakes up.
I need that moment.
Time sometimes evaporates,
like the morning breeze
filtering through the balcony screen door.
Important things,
like writing,
playing,
sharing,
take a back seat
to the functional,
monotonous
chores of the day.
In that quiet moment
one can reflect,
without ambient noise and distraction,
on that which is good in the world.
The quiet allows
for decisions to be made,
and growth to happen.

A Beautiful Day

Today is
a beautiful day,
moderate temperature,
gorgeous blue sky,
white lambs wool clouds
sporadically wiping it clean.

The sun trickles
down through the trees,
one leaf at a time,
like white rain,
until it reaches the grass,
illuminating everything
it touches
and painting shadows.

A child's laughter
echoes through
the quiet,
chasing the cottonwood seeds
riding on the breeze,
searching for a place
to land.

Picnic in the Woods

Spring was late that year.
Walking into the woods,
a gray cloud canopy overhead,
we entered a black and white world,
void of color,
sometimes with sepia filters.

Snow was gone,
undergrowth just a thought
beneath broken leaves that blanketed the ground.
Naked trees filled the woods.
A perfect environment
for wandering off the path.

A fallen log near a small creek
became a bench as our picnic unfolded -
peanut butter sandwiches,
carrot sticks, cheese and water.

Reflections of the trees
rippled as the breeze skimmed
across the creek's surface,
and whispered in the tree tops.

Politics of spring were visible
in the dance of the birds.
A few duck couples were near,
some grazing in a small pond,
white bottoms pointing to the sky.

White shelf mushrooms
dotted bark stripped trees,
a sign of decomposition.

The quiet calm allowed details
to imprint in my mind,
challenging me to use my imagination,
to look beyond structure,
to see.

My Sanctuary

Home to squirrels, nuthatches and wood peckers,
large maple trees - one, two, three - shade my back yard.

So much shade only ferns, hostas, wild violets
and creeping charlie care to grow.

While branches are naked, spring daffodils and
bleeding heart sprinkle the ground under the south tree.

A nuthatch takes up residence in a small hole
in the oldest maple, the abandoned home of a red squirrel.

Critters are abundant above ground, and below,
chipmunks, moles, voles, bunnies and coyotes.

Disheveled wood piles near a broken block fire ring
hold branches from God's winter pruning.

It may not look like much, but there is
so much life in my back yard.

Siting here, on the porch, I can't help but smile,
a silent observer in the sanctuary I call home.

Beauty of Perceptions

Memories are God's strings
that attach us together.
My memories
are mine
though the strings
of my perceptions
intersect with others,
creating bold
colorful
string art images.

Home

Silence,
my purposeful steps
on the trail
the only sound,
meadow on one side,
the river on the other.

A small golden doe
stands between me
and the river,
neck extended,
ears propped at attention,
assessing.
Deciding I am a threat
she lopes off.

Stepping into the forest
a breeze whispers
through the trees.
Grandfather Oak
stretches his arms above me
sheltering me
with his strength.
Looking up
blue sky peeks through
the gnarled fingers
splattered with green leaves.

Tiny dragonflies
perch on thin fingers
of a lifeless arm,
one,
and then another,
and then another,
until there are five,
comfortable with my presence,
watching my every move.

The forest
is beautiful here,
the thin underbrush
speckled with
the suns' kiss.
I dance
through the trees
with the wind
and the sun,
my arms in the air
a grin on my face.

I am home.

What are You Going to Leave this World?

If I could
I would leave you
seeds of hope,
and a sail
to catch the wind
of blessings.

I would leave strings of words
that provoke thought,
empower,
and share the joy
of tomorrow.

I would leave dandelion seeds
floating in the air
like glitter
with sunlight shining
through them.

I would help you see
the intricacies
of breath,
and life
to understand
a higher power.

I would leave the knowledge
of generosity
through love
because of love

For now,
I leave prisms
hanging in my windows
for the sun to paint
rainbow promises
on my walls
and I ponder:

Will I leave the world
a better place
because I was here?

Words have been a part of **Gail Lipe's** life since she was little. She wrote her first short stories in elementary school and has continued writing throughout her life. Poetry helped keep her sane through her tumultuous teen-age years, and prose and journalism were her bread and butter for many years as an adult. She was a staff writer/photographer for a community newspaper for about 10 years and was a freelance columnist and reporter at different papers for several years before and after that.

The inspiration for Lipe's poetry comes from her deep feelings about life, her faith in God, and the abundant details in nature. Her view of life's gifts, and turmoils, bleeds onto the page with every word.

An eclectic artist, Lipe has merged words and art together in handmade book structures, pottery and many more ideas yet to be created.

She loves her family, and the outdoors, where her soul is fed. She feels privileged to live in Minnesota where seasons change and where a variety of landforms can be found within a few hours drive.

Lipe published a biography about her mother titled *No Time to Quit: Life in a Broken Package*, a fiction piece titled *Things Change* in The Jackpine Writers' Bloc *The Talking Stick Volume 25*, a poem titled *water's journey* in The Jackpine Writers' Bloc *The Talking Stick Volume 33 Earth Signs*, and a fiction piece titled *The Hunt* in *The RavensPerch*. She also participates in readings of her poetry and short stories.

www.ingramcontent.com/pod-product-compliance
Lightning Source LLC
Chambersburg PA
CBHW030058170426
43197CB00010B/1582